HEALTHY CHRISTMAS SNACKS AND DESSERTS RECIPES FOR CHILDREN

Christmas Desserts and Snacks to Prepare for Children

TABLE OF CONTENTS

INTRODUCTION

CHRISTMAS SNACKS AND DESSERT

Christmas is the festival of the year. The family comes together and everything should be perfect. So that nothing goes wrong, you will find delicious starters, main dishes and desserts for the Christmas menu as well as recipe ideas for a festive Christmas brunch. We wish you wonderful holidays with your loved ones!

A refined starter, an elaborate main course and a special dessert: Christmas dinner is not spilled, but padded! On the holidays you can feast with a clear conscience. It starts with the traditional Christmas dinner on December 24th. and runs through the rest of the holidays. Let yourself be inspired by our delicious recipe ideas for starters, main courses and desserts!

The crowning glory of a delicious Christmas menu is a delicious dessert and snacks: have you ever tried baked apple tiramisu? The combination of baked apple and tiramisu is unbeatably delicious! Or is a crème brulée seasoned for Christmas more your taste? Whether a simple crumble or fine cinnamon parfait with port wine pears, here are our best Christmas desserts.

Christmas desserts and snacks to prepare for children

In addition to the Christmas dessert classics are layer desserts easy and delicious choice. You can prepare these very well, as you usually only need a few ingredients for them. Trifles are great for a Christmas in a larger group, as you can layer the ingredients nicely in a large glass jar. Semifreddo, or parfait, and ice cream are also very easy to prepare, as they usually have to freeze for a night. Our highlight is the coconut semifreddo with passion fruit. Exotic and beautifully Christmassy!

With our recipes for preparing Christmas desserts, you will also save yourself more stress in the kitchen on the holiday.

Our Christmas snacks and desserts not only taste nice and sweet, they also contain healthy ingredients - the perfect mix for everyone who doesn't want to go without a snacks and dessert for a party, but still want to stay slim and fit. We wish you a lot of fun while enjoying and a Merry Christmas!

RECIPES

Simple, juicy chocolate cake

preparation

10 min.

baking time

55 min.

ingredients

- 300 grams of butter soft
- 180 grams of sugar
- 5 medium-sized eggs
- 150 grams of wheat flour
- 150 grams of ground almonds or hazelnuts
- 2 teaspoons of baking powder
- 1 pinch of salt
- 50 grams of cocoa
- 80 grams of grated chocolate
- 250 grams of chocolate icing rough specification

preparation

1. Preheat the oven to 180 degrees top and bottom heat. Grease a large box cake tin (approx. 28 cm) and dust with flour. Alternatively, you can also use a springform pan, but the baking time may then have to be adjusted.
2. For the dough, beat the softened butter with the sugar until frothy, stir in the eggs one at a time. Slowly add the flour mixed with the almonds, baking powder, salt and baking cocoa; Finally fold in the grated chocolate.

3. Pour the dough into the prepared pan and smooth it out. Bake for about 50 to 60 minutes. Make a chopstick test. The cake can (and should) be a little moist inside. Let the cake cool in the pan, then turn it out. Cover with chocolate icing.

Fanta cake from the tray with sour cream and peaches

preparation

30 min.

baking time

25 min.

waiting period

1 hour

Quantity: 1 baking sheet

ingredients

For the dough

- 4 medium-sized eggs
- 180 grams of sugar
- 350 grams of wheat flour
- 1 packet of baking powder
- 130 milliliters of oil
- 170 milliliters of Fanta or other orange lemonade

For covering

- 600 milliliters of cream
- 3 packets of cream stabilizer
- 2 packets of vanilla sugar
- 1 tablespoon of sugar
- 500 grams of sour cream
- 1 large can of peaches approx. 450 g drained weight, or fresh and peeled

preparation

1. Preheat the oven to 175 degrees top and bottom heat. Beat the eggs with the sugar for a few minutes until frothy. Stir in the flour mixed with the baking powder alternately with the oil. Finally add the lemonade, but then don't stir too long so that the carbonic acid does not escape.
2. Spread the dough on a greased tray and bake for about 25-30 minutes. Let cool down.
3. In the meantime, peel the fruit for the topping (for fresh peaches) or allow it to drain. Cut into small cubes.
4. Whip the cream with the whipped cream and vanilla sugar until stiff. Mix the sour cream with the sugar until smooth and fold in the whipped cream with the fruit.
5. Spread the sour cream on the cooled cake base; if you don't have a deep tray, it's best to put a baking frame around it. Chill the Fanta cake for approx. 1 hour (alternatively overnight) and dust with cinnamon sugar or gold dust before eating.

Mole cake with banana and cherries

preparation

30 min.

baking time

30 min.

waiting period

1 hour

Quantity: 1 springform pan (approx. 18 cm)

ingredients

For base and crumble

- 75 grams of butter soft
- 90 grams of sugar
- 3 large eggs
- 100 grams of wheat flour
- 2 teaspoons of baking powder
- 2 teaspoons of cocoa
- 30 grams of grated chocolate, preferably dark

For the filling

- 1 large banana
- 150 grams of cherries fresh and pitted or out of the glass
- 300 milliliters of cream chilled
- 1 packet of vanilla sugar
- 2 packets of cream stabilizer
- 30 grams of grated chocolate
- 1 tablespoon of baking cocoa for dusting

preparation

1. Preheat the oven to 180 degrees top and bottom heat. Grease a small springform pan and dust with a little flour.
2. Beat the softened butter with the sugar until frothy, stir in the eggs one by one. Stir in the flour mixed with baking powder and cocoa together with the chocolate shavings. Pour the dough into the mold and bake for about 30 minutes. Let cool down.
3. Place the cake base on a plate or plate and scoop out with a tablespoon. Leave a small margin (approx. 1 cm). The bottom should not be hollowed out too deep so that it remains reasonably stable for the filling. Crumble the scraped pieces of pastry into a bowl.
4. Halve the banana lengthways and place on the edge in the hollowed-out ground. Drain the cherries and distribute them in the middle.
5. Beat the cream with the vanilla sugar until stiff, then stir in the cream stiffener towards the end. Fold the chocolate shavings into the whipped cream.
6. Spread the cream on the cake base in a dome shape. Go almost to the edge. Sprinkle the cake with the crumbles and press them down a little if necessary. Chill the cake for at least 1 hour and dust with baking cocoa before serving.

Simple banana cake recipe with delicious variations

preparation

10 min.

baking time

45 min.

Quantity: 1 kl. Bundt pan (20 cm)

ingredients

- 200 grams of butter soft
- 120 grams of brown sugar
- 4 medium-sized eggs
- 2 ripe bananas approx. 250g
- 300 grams of wheat flour
- 2 teaspoons of baking powder
- 1 pinch of salt
- 2 tablespoons of milk as needed
- Icing sugar or couverture to decorate

preparation

1. Preheat the oven to 175 degrees top and bottom heat. A small Grease a bundt pan with a diameter of approx. 20 cm and sprinkle with a little flour. Mix the softened butter with the sugar for a few minutes until frothy. Stir in the eggs one by one.

2. Process the ripe bananas into puree with a fork or hand blender. Stir into the egg and butter cream. Add the flour and salt mixed with the baking powder. Stir everything. If the dough is too firm, add a little milk.
3. Pour the batter into the tin, smooth it out and bake for approx. 45 minutes. Make a chopstick test. Turn the cake out and decorate it with powdered sugar, couverture or something similar.

Simple and ingeniously juicy chocolate sheet cake

preparation

10 min.

baking time

35 min.

Quantity: 1 tray

ingredients

For the dough

- 250 grams of butter soft
- 220 grams of brown sugar
- 3 medium-sized eggs
- 450 grams of wheat flour
- 60 grams of baking cocoa
- 1/2 packet of baking powder
- 3/4 teaspoon baking soda
- 1 pinch of salt
- 400 milliliters of buttermilk

For decoration

- 200 grams of chocolate icing
- Sugar sprinkles

preparation

1. Preheat the oven to 175 degrees top and bottom heat. Cover a tray with baking paper or grease and dust with flour. Beat the soft butter with the (brown) sugar until frothy. Mix in eggs one at a time.
2. Mix the flour, cocoa, baking powder, baking soda and salt. Alternate with the buttermilk, stir briefly but vigorously into the egg mixture. Spread the dough on the baking sheet and smooth it out. Bake for around 35 minutes.
3. Let the cake cool down. Spread with chocolate icing or couverture and decorate the sprinkles.

Super juicy fizzy cake from the tray

preparation

15 min.

baking time

20 min.

Quantity: 1 baking sheet

ingredients

For the dough

- 180 grams of powdered sugar or more to taste
- 5 medium-sized eggs
- 170 grams of butter liquid
- 200 grams of wheat flour
- 100 grams of ground almonds

- 2 packets of vanilla custard powder or 80g cornstarch
- 1 packet of baking powder
- 1 teaspoon vanilla paste or 1 mark
- 170 milliliters of mineral water with plenty of sparkling water

For the casting

- 200 grams of powdered sugar
- 5 tablespoons of milk as a rough indication
- Sugar sprinkles as desired

preparation

1. Preheat the oven to 175 degrees top and bottom heat. Line a baking sheet with parchment paper. Beat the eggs and powdered sugar for a few minutes until very lightly. Mix the flour with the almonds, baking powder and pudding powder.
2. Do not stir dry ingredients into the egg mixture for too long, alternating with the oil and vanilla pulp. At the end, stir in the sparkling water only briefly and carefully so that the carbon dioxide remains in the dough. Bake the cake for around 20 minutes.
3. Let the cake cool down. For the thin topping, stir sifted powdered sugar with enough milk until you get a tough but spreadable mixture. Spread on the cake and decorate with sugar decorations.

Fried egg cake with apricots for Christmas

preparation

25 min.

baking time

20 min.

Quantity: 1 tray

ingredients

For the dough

- 200 grams of butter soft
- 180 grams of sugar
- 5 medium-sized eggs
- 300 grams of wheat flour
- 3 teaspoons of baking powder
- 5 tablespoons of milk as a rough indication

For cream cheese cream

- 150 grams of butter soft
- 180 grams of powdered sugar
- 400 grams of cream cheese creamy
- 1 tablespoon lemon juice or lemon zest as desired

For decoration

- 1 can of apricots approx. 500g drained weight
- 1 1/2 packets of cake topping
- 3 tablespoons of sugar
- 350 milliliters of water, possibly half of the apricot juice from the can

preparation

1. For the batter base, beat soft butter until frothy, gradually add the sugar and eggs and keep stirring. Preheat the oven to 175 degrees top and bottom heat.
2. Mix flour with baking powder and stir into the mixture. Add milk so that the cake batter falls from the spoon and tears.
3. Place the batter on a greased tray or a baking sheet lined with baking paper, smooth the surface and bake for 20-25 minutes. Let cool down.
4. For the cream cheese frosting, beat soft butter until frothy, gradually pour in powdered sugar. Stir in the cream cheese and flavor it with lemon zest or lemon juice, for example.
5. Spread the topping on the cooled dough sheet. Drain the apricots from the can, collecting the juice. Cut the cake into pieces and put one halved apricot in the middle. Lightly press.
6. Mix the icing powder with sugar and stir in 350 ml of liquid. Heat. Carefully cool slightly on the cake, so spread the frosting including the apricots. Let it set and cut the pieces again with a sharp knife.

Healthy apple and carrot cake without sugar

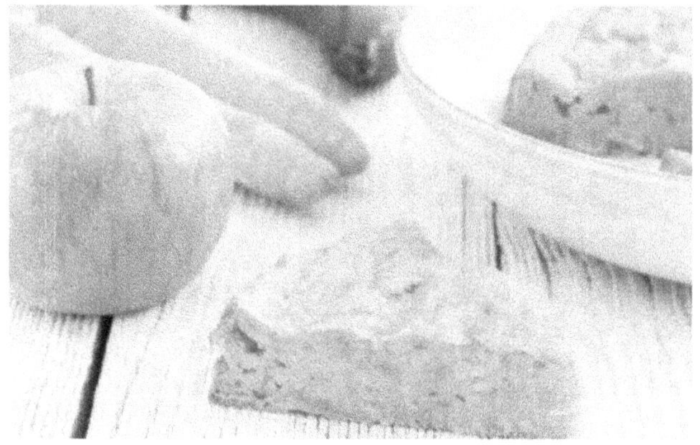

preparation

15 min.

baking time

40 min.

Quantity: 1 kl. Springform pan (20 cm)

Ingredients

- 100 grams of carrots finely grated or grated, weighed cleaned
- 100 grams of apples finely grated or grated, weighed cleaned
- 130 grams of banana must be very ripe and sweet
- 1 medium-sized egg
- 80 grams of Greek yogurt, alternatively sour cream
- 40 grams of coconut oil liquid, alternatively 60g butter
- 2 teaspoons of cinnamon
- 1 piece of vanilla pod
- 1 pinch of salt
- 1 teaspoon lemon juice
- 130 grams of wheat flour e.g., spelled flour 630 or whole grain
- 1 teaspoon of baking powder

preparation

1. Grate or grate the carrot and apple very finely. Puree the banana into the pulp. Put aside.
2. Preheat the oven to 175 degrees top and bottom heat. Whisk the egg with the yogurt, stir in coconut oil. Mix the remaining dry ingredients and add to the wet ingredients. Mix in briefly but thoroughly. Finally stir in the prepared fruit (puree).
3. Grease the small springform pan and dust with flour or line with baking paper. Pour in the dough and smooth out. Bake the cake for about 40 minutes. Best kept in the refrigerator.

Apple pie without sugar, butter, milk and egg

preparation

15 min.

baking time

40 min.

Quantity: 1 kl. Springform pan (approx. 20cm)

ingredients

- 200 grams of spelled flour type 630, alternatively wheat flour
- 1 teaspoon of baking powder
- 1/2 teaspoon of baking soda
- 50 grams ground almonds
- 1/2 teaspoon of cinnamon
- 1/2 piece of vanilla pulp half scraped out pod
- 150 milliliters of oat milk or almond, rice or cow milk
- 1/2 teaspoon apple cider vinegar
- 150 grams of banana puree, apple and banana pulp or date puree
- 1 tablespoon coconut oil, alternatively rapeseed oil or similar
- 300 grams of apples

preparation

1. Wash, peel and core the apples and cut into small pieces. Preheat the oven to 175 degrees top and bottom heat. Grease a small springform pan (20-22 cm) or line it with baking paper.

2. Mix the flour, baking powder, baking soda, almonds, cinnamon and vanilla. In a second bowl, mix the oat milk with the vinegar, fruit puree and coconut oil so that there are no more pieces.
3. Briefly but vigorously stir the liquid ingredients into the dry ingredients. Fold in the apple pieces. Pour the dough into the pan and smooth it out.
4. Bake cakes for 40-45 minutes. Possibly do a chopstick test. The cake is quite juicy on the inside, but of course it should be baked through. Warm it tastes more like a casserole; If left in the refrigerator overnight, it will become firmer.

Healthy baby spelled sticks without sugar

preparation

10 min.

baking time

25 min.

Quantity: 25 small bars

ingredients

- 220 grams of spelled flour type 630
- 50 milliliters of rapeseed oil
- 1 small banana very ripe, approx. 100g. about 80g pulp
- 1 piece of apples approx. 150g, of which approx. 90g is pulp

preparation

1. Finely mash the ripe banana with a fork. Peel and grate the apple. Knead both with the flour and oil to form a dough.
2. Preheat the oven to 180 degrees top and bottom heat. Cover a tray with baking paper. Shape the dough into long, thin rolls, cut off long pieces with a sharp knife and shape them into tips at the ends. Bake the snack sticks for about 25 minutes.

Healthy muesli bars without baking: vegan & sugar-free

preparation

10 min.

Soaking time

10 min.

Quantity: 15 bars

Ingredients

- 120 grams of soft dates or fresh ones
- 100 grams of muesli mix or 5-grain flakes
- 100 grams of tender oatmeal
- 60 grams of nuts, kernels or almonds to taste
- 80 grams of agave syrup or honey / rice syrup
- 130 grams of almond butter or nut butter

preparation

1. Pour some hot water over the dates and let them soak for around 10 minutes.
2. Mix the muesli mix, oat flakes and chopped nuts, almonds or kernels.
3. Puree the dates together with a little of the soaking water in a kitchen chopper or similar to a fine purée.
4. Mix the sweetener and nut butter until smooth. If both are too firm, simply heat them up briefly. Mix with the dry ingredients and the date butter. Knead everything well.
5. Refine the muesli mixture as you like (see tips). Place in a small tin lined with baking paper (max. 20 * 30 cm). Press firmly and leave in the refrigerator. Cut into bars with a sharp knife.

Make your own fruit bars without sugar

preparation

15 min.

Cooling time

2 hours

Quantity: 15 bars

ingredients

- 200 grams of soft dates
- 180 grams of dried fruits see tips
- 180 grams of nuts, kernels or almonds see tips
- 4 large square wafers optional, 100 * 150 cm

preparation

1. Put dates, fruits, nuts or kernels in a powerful food processor and process into a homogeneous, sticky mass. If you want the bars to be fine without bits, just grind the nuts first.
2. Line a small mold (approx. 30 * 20 cm) with cling film, distribute the mixture on the floor and smooth it out. To do this, keep dipping the scraper or cake spatula in water.
3. Place the foil on the surface and weigh down the mass a little. Chill for at least 1 to 2 hours.
4. Peel off the foil and turn the plate onto a board. Place large square wafers on top and press firmly. Turnover and press wafers on the other side as well. Cut into bars with a large, sharp knife. This is easier if you cut one side of the wafer beforehand.

Healthy muesli cookies: vegan, low-fat & crispy

preparation

10 min.

baking time

22 min.

Quantity: 30 pieces

Ingredients

For the basic dough

- 120 grams of fruit puree e.g., apple or apple-strawberry puree
- 90 grams of agave syrup or honey, maple syrup or rice syrup
- 2 1/2 tablespoons of sunflower oil
- 1 pinch of salt
- 1 pinch of ground vanilla
- 200 grams of tender oatmeal !
- 100 grams of wheat flour, preferably type 550
- To refine
- 40 grams of nuts, kernels or almonds e.g., sunflower kernels, flax seeds
- 50 grams of dried fruits e.g., cranberries, cherries, apricots
- 1 teaspoon lemon juice optional

preparation

1. Preheat the oven to 175 degrees top and bottom heat. Line two trays with baking paper. Whisk the moist ingredients - fruit puree, sweetener and oil.
2. Mix the remaining dry ingredients and stir with a wooden spoon or spatula under the damp. Either mix the entire amount of dough with (chopped) dried fruits, kernels, seeds and the like, or divide it up and make different types of biscuits.
3. Shape the dough into small balls with your hands; if the mixture is very moist, just add a teaspoon of flour. Flatten the balls, for example with a spatula, and distribute the cookies on the baking sheets. Bake cookies for 12 minutes, then turn and bake for another 10-12 minutes. Proceed in the same way with the second sheet.

Applesauce muffins for babies without sugar, egg, butter or flour

preparation

5 min.

baking time

20 min.

Quantity: 8 muffins

ingredients

For the muffins

- 350 grams of apple sauce without sugar, rather firm
- 50 grams of millet flakes
- 50 grams of almond flour

preparation

1. Preheat the oven to 180 degrees top and bottom heat. Mix the applesauce with millet flakes and almond flour. Either use the dough as it is or refine it further (see tips). Fill the batter into silicone muffin cups. Bake for around 20 minutes.

Homemade crackers in just 15 minutes

preparation

7 min.

baking time

8 min.

Quantity: 30 pieces

ingredients

- 150 grams of spelled flour type 630, alternatively normal wheat flour
- 1/2 teaspoon of salt
- 40 grams of butter very cold and in pieces
- 70 milliliters of milk
- Seasoned salt for sprinkling

preparation

2. Preheat the oven to 220 degrees top and bottom heat. Cover a tray with baking paper. Put the flour and salt in a bowl.
3. Add the cold butter in small pieces and the milk and quickly knead all the ingredients to form a smooth dough. Roll out thinly on a lightly floured work surface or baking mat, cut small crackers with a pastry wheel.
4. Place crackers on the baking sheet, sprinkle with seasoned salt and bake for 8-10 minutes, depending on the thickness.

Nibble rolls or bread for babies and toddlers

preparation

15 min.

baking time

25 min.

waiting period

1 hour 30 minutes

Quantity: 20 small rolls

ingredients

For the yeast dough

- 400 grams of spelled flour type 630
- 1 packet of dry yeast
- 80 milliliters of orange juice or apple juice
- 80 milliliters of lukewarm water
- 50 grams of rapeseed oil
- 100 grams of grated apples
- 100 grams of grated carrots
- To refine
- 2 tablespoons of raisins optional
- 2 tablespoons of rice syrup or other sweetness, optional

- To wallow
- 50 grams of oatmeal

preparation

1. Put the flour, dry yeast, juice, water, oil and possibly sweetener in a bowl. Mix and knead for a few minutes with the food processor or the dough hook of the hand mixer. Cover the dough and let it rise in a warm place for 30 minutes.
2. Squeeze out the grated apple and carrot a little. Knead under the dough; Add raisins if desired. Cover and let rise again in a warm place for 1 hour.
3. Preheat the oven to 200 degrees top and bottom heat. Line a baking sheet with parchment paper. Shape the dough into balls with your hands and roll them in the oat flakes, then place them on the baking tray with a little space. Bake for around 25 minutes. When fresh, the rolls are still quite damp; that changes after a few hours. They're also easy to freeze.

Vegan banana and oat muffins without sugar or fat

preparation

5 min.

baking time

20 min.

Quantity: 10 muffins

ingredients

- 3 large bananas very ripe, approx. 450 grams with the skin
- 120 milliliters of oat milk

- 120 grams of spelled flour
- 80 grams of tender oatmeal
- 2 teaspoons of baking powder
- 1 teaspoon of cinnamon
- 1 teaspoon lemon juice
- 1 piece of vanilla pulp, scraped out pulp of a pod, optional

preparation

1. Preheat the oven to 180 degrees top and bottom heat. Puree the very ripe bananas to make puree. First stir in the oat milk, then the remaining ingredients vigorously, but not for too long.
2. Fill dough into muffin molds (preferably made of silicone, the muffins may stick in paper molds). Bake for around 20 minutes.

Savory muffins with vegetables and cheese

preparation

10 min.

baking time

25 min.

Quantity: 12 muffins

ingredients

For the dough

- 300 grams of wheat flour

- 1 teaspoon of salt
- 2 1/2 teaspoons of baking powder
- 2 medium-sized eggs
- 250 milliliters of milk
- 80 grams of butter melted

To refine

- 1/2 piece of paprika
- 40 grams of peas, preferably frozen
- 40 grams frozen corn or can
- 80 grams of feta or other cheese

preparation

1. First prepare the vegetables and cheese: wash, clean and halve the pepper; Cut one half into small cubes. Thaw or drain the peas and corn. Cut or crumble the cheese into small cubes.
2. Preheat the oven to 190 degrees top and bottom heat. Mix the dry muffin ingredients in a bowl. Mix eggs, milk and melted butter in another bowl. Add the moist to the dry ingredients and stir briefly (!) But vigorously. Fold the vegetables and cheese into the batter.
3. Fill the dough into 12 paper or silicone molds and ideally place them in a muffin tin. Bake muffins for about 25-30 minutes. They taste lukewarm, but also very good cold.

Make energy bars yourself (flapjacks or energy bars)

preparation

10 min.

baking time

24 min.

Quantity: 15 pieces

ingredients

- 150 grams of butter
- 140 grams of rice syrup or honey or agave syrup
- 70 grams of coconut blossom sugar or brown sugar
- 270 grams of tender oatmeal
- 80 grams of sunflower seeds or other seeds and nuts
- 70 grams of dried cranberries or raisins, dates, etc.

preparation

1. Preheat the oven to 175 degrees top and bottom heat. Melt the butter in a saucepan. Add the syrup or honey and sugar and stir until the sugar has dissolved.
2. Take the pot off the stove. Stir the oat flakes well into the mixture. Fold in nuts, kernels, seeds and dried fruits as desired.
3. Put the mixture in a rectangular shape lined with baking paper (at least 20 * 20 cm) and press firmly with a spatula or spoon. Bake for around 23-25 minutes. While still warm, use a sharp knife to carefully "cut" around 15 bars so that they can be cut more easily later. Let it cool down, for example in the refrigerator, and then cut through it completely.

Healthy donuts: vegan, sugar-free & naturally colored

preparation

20 min.

baking time

15 min.

Quantity: 6 pieces Calories: 178 kcal

ingredients

For the dough

- 70 grams of apple sauce without sugar
- 20 grams of coconut oil
- 180 milliliters of oat milk
- 1/2 teaspoon lemon juice
- 120 grams of spelled flour type 630
- 50 grams of ground almonds
- 1 teaspoon of baking soda
- 40 grams of erythritol optional, see tips

For the glaze

- 200 grams of white chocolate without sugar vegan see tips
- 1 teaspoon coconut oil
- Eat a rainbow colors
- Decorating ideas
- Desiccated coconut
- Cocoa nibs
- freeze-dried raspberries
- Banana chips
- chopped almonds

preparation

1. Preheat the oven to 175 degrees top and bottom heat. Whisk applesauce, liquid oil and oat milk together (careful, it may splash). Mix the dry ingredients. Mix briefly but vigorously with the liquid ingredients.
2. Fill the dough with a small spoon or piping bag into a donut mold, preferably made of silicone. Shake gently until smooth and bake the donuts for about 13-15 minutes. Take out of the mold and let cool down.
3. For the glaze, chop the white chocolate and melt it together with the oil in a hot water bath; if the mixture is still too tough, add another teaspoon of oil. Distribute in as many bowls as you want colors. Put one kind of Eat a Rainbow powder in each bowl and stir in very well. It is best to start with 1/2 teaspoon and then add more and more until the desired color is achieved.
4. Spread the chocolate over the donuts with a spoon; alternatively, dip the donuts upside down. Decorate with chopped almonds, berries, cocoa nibs, desiccated coconut or similar and let set. Store in a Tupperware box and eat as fresh as possible; but they can also be frozen.

Mini pancake skewers with fruit and chocolate cream

preparation

15 min.

baking time

5 min.

waiting period

10 min.

Quantity: 25 pieces

Ingredients

For the pancakes

- 150 milliters of buttermilk
- 100 grams of natural yogurt
- 2 medium-sized eggs
- 1 tablespoon of coconut oil
- 200 grams of spelled flour type 630, part whole grain is also possible
- 1/2 teaspoon of baking soda
- 1 teaspoon of baking powder
- 2 tablespoons coconut blossom sugar amount as desired
- For the nut cream
- 200 grams of hazelnuts
- 3 tablespoons of coconut oil

- 2 teaspoons of cocoa
- 50 grams of Loacker waffles Napolitaner or cream cocoa
- 1 tablespoon coconut blossom sugar optional
- For the almond cream
- 200 grams of peeled almonds
- 3 tablespoons of coconut oil
- 50 grams of Loacker vanilla wafers

For the skewers

- 60 grams of Loacker waffles Napolitaner, cream cocoa or vanilla
- Fruit e.g., berries, grapes, banana, kiwi

preparation

1. First prepare the creams (see notes). To do this, roast the nuts for about 8 minutes at 170 degrees top and bottom heat, the almonds are best used unroasted. Put the hazelnuts in a powerful food processor or kitchen chopper and grind very finely to a paste; it takes a few minutes. Mix in coconut oil, cocoa, sugar and half of the waffles. Fold in the remaining waffles, finely chopped, as a crunch. Use the same principle to make a light cream from the almonds.
2. For the pancakes, whisk the buttermilk with the yogurt, eggs and coconut oil. Mix the flour with baking soda, baking powder and coconut sugar. Mix with the egg cream to a smooth batter. Let rest for 5-10 minutes.
3. Heat a large non-stick pan. Pour in some (coconut) oil. Add 1-2 teaspoons of batter for a mini pancake to the pan and bake on both sides over medium heat. Several pancakes fit in one large pan. At the end there should be around 50 mini pancakes for 25 skewers.
4. Cut out the pancakes with a round cookie cutter (approx. 4 cm) so that they are evenly sized. Cut the waffles into small squares with a sharp knife. Put on small wooden skewers with fruits and 0.5-1 teaspoon each of chocolate cream.

Bake breadsticks yourself: simple snack sticks

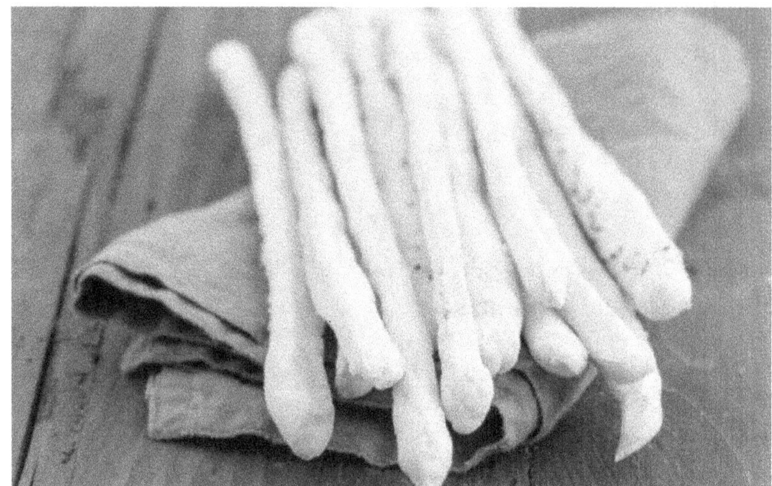

preparation

10 min.

baking time

12 min.

waiting period

45 min.

Quantity: 30 pieces

Ingredients

- 250 grams of wheat flour type 550 or double-handle flour
- 1/2 packet of dry yeast alternatively 1/4 cube fresh
- 1 pinch of sugar
- 125 milliliters of lukewarm water
- 2 tablespoons of olive oil
- 3/4 teaspoon salt

preparation

1. Mix the flour and dry yeast. Mix together with all the other ingredients briefly on the lowest setting, then knead (let) for about 5 minutes until the dough is smooth and comes off the edge of the bowl.
2. Cover the bowl with cling film and let the dough rise in a warm place for about 45 minutes.

3. Preheat the oven to 180 degrees top and bottom heat. Line two trays with baking paper. Knead the dough again briefly and roll it out thickly on a lightly floured work surface.
4. Cut the dough into narrow strips with a sharp knife and shape them into thin rolls; alternatively, remove small portions of dough and form rolls directly. The thinner the breadsticks, the crispier they will be.
5. Spread the breadsticks on the baking sheets with a little space between them. Brush lightly with water and sprinkle with coarse salt, sesame, spices, herbs or the like. Bake for about 12-15 minutes, depending on the thickness.

Healthy vegan children's biscuits without sugar and eggs

preparation

10 min.

baking time

20 min.

Quantity: 35 cookies

ingredients

- 1 1/2 large apples peeled and grated
- 1 tablespoon of lemon juice
- 120 grams of dried apricots unsulphurized
- 90 milliliters of oat milk, alternatively cow, almond or rice milk
- 90 milliliters of coconut oil or rapeseed oil, I use a 1: 1 mixture

- 270 grams of whole wheat flour or whole spelled
- 180 grams of 5-grain mixture, alternatively just oat flakes
- 1 pinch of salt

preparation

1. Drizzle the grated apples with the lemon juice. Chop the apricots very finely and add. Preheat the oven to 180 degrees top and bottom heat.
2. Mix the milk and oil. Put the flour, flakes, salt and possibly spices in a bowl. Quickly stir in the fruits and the milk-oil mixture (you can also use a simple spatula). The dough should be rather moist. If it is extremely wet, you can add a spoonful of flour.
3. Form small balls with your hands, place them on a baking sheet lined with baking paper and flatten the balls into biscuits. The thinner the batter, the crisper the cookies will be. Bake cookies for about 20 minutes. They tend to stay soft.

Vegan apricot and coconut balls without sugar

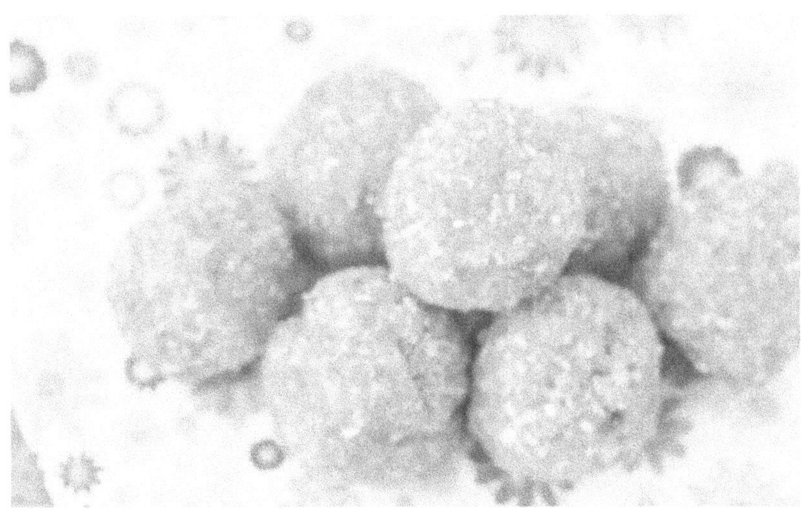

preparation

5 min.

Quantity: 15 balls

ingredients

- 120 grams of dried apricots
- 20 grams of almonds blanched and ground

- 30 grams of desiccated coconut
- 1 pinch of salt
- 1/2 teaspoon vanilla flavor liquid

preparation

1. Put all ingredients in the food processor and mix until they are nicely chopped up and not quite as chunky. Alternatively, use a good hand blender or kitchen shredder. Form small balls with your hands.

Low carb vanilla crescents without sugar and flour

preparation

10 min.

baking time

10 min.

waiting period

30 min.

Quantity: 40 pieces

Ingredients

For the normal croissants

- 150 grams of almond flour, de-oiled, light variant
- 75 grams of ground almonds blanched
- 120 grams of butter soft
- 40 grams of xylitol
- 40 grams of erythritol
- 2 medium egg yolks
- 1/2 teaspoon baking powder
- 1/2 piece of vanilla pulp from half a pod
- 1 pinch of salt
- Icing sugar made from erythritol
- Also, for the protein croissants
- 50 grams of protein powder organic & vanilla (see instructions in the recipe!)

preparation

2. Mix the dry ingredients in a bowl with the exception of the powder xucker. In a second bowl, beat the softened butter with the sweeteners until frothy, then stir in the egg yolks one by one.
3. Add the almond mixture to the moist ingredients and knead everything into a comparatively soft dough. Shape the dough into a kind of ball and wrap it in cling film and let it cool for about 30 minutes.
4. Preheat the oven to 175 degrees top and bottom heat. Press the dough portion by portion into the wells of a vanilla biscuit mold and remove the excess dough with a sharp knife. Alternatively, shape into thin rolls with your hands, cut and shape into croissants with pointed ends.
5. Bake the vanilla crescents for about 10-12 minutes. Let cool briefly in the tin, carefully remove and roll in the powder xucker while it is still hot. Careful: the croissants can be a bit fragile.

Fast low carb cookies without flour or sugar

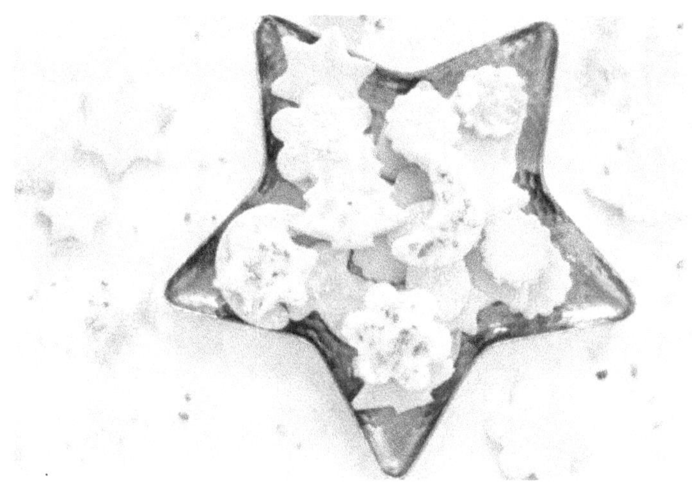

preparation

15 min.

baking time

10 min.

Cooling time

30 min.

Quantity: 60 pieces

Ingredients

- 300 grams of almonds ground and blanched
- 1 large egg
- 60 grams of butter soft
- 40 grams of xylitol ground very finely
- 40 grams of erythritol ground very finely, e.g., powder xucker

preparation

1. Knead all the ingredients for the dough together. Xylitol and erythritol should be powdery or at least finely ground.
2. Wrap the dough in foil and cool for about 30 minutes.
3. Preheat the oven to 175 degrees top and bottom heat. Roll out the dough between two layers of foil or on a baking mat sprinkled with almonds. Cut out shapes. Place the cookies on a baking tray lined with baking paper and bake for about 10 minutes.

Low carb cinnamon stars without sugar

preparation

15 min.

baking time

25 min.

waiting period

30 min.

Quantity: 60 pieces

Ingredients

- 3 medium-sized egg whites
- 150 grams of erythritol powder xucker
- 350 grams ground almonds
- 1 teaspoon of cinnamon
- 2 drops of bitter almond oil

preparation

1. Beat the egg whites until stiff. Add the sifted Sukrin Melis tablespoon at a time. Set aside about 5 tablespoons of the egg whites for the topping of the cinnamon stars. Preheat the stove to 120 degrees.
2. Mix the ground almonds with the cinnamon and bitter almond oil. With a spatula or wooden spoon carefully lift gabz under the egg whites so that the air stays in the egg whites and it doesn't collapse completely.
3. Place the dough in the refrigerator for about half an hour and then roll it out, either between cling film or on a baking mat, about half a centimeter thick. You can sprinkle some ground almonds on the work surface if the dough is too sticky.
4. Cut stars out of the dough and place on a baking tray lined with baking paper. Spread the ice cream mass on the stars. Bake or dry in a preheated oven at 120 degrees for about 20-25 minutes.

Low carb rascals without flour and sugar

preparation

15 min.

baking time

10 min.

Quantity: 12 pieces

ingredients

For the dough

- 60 grams of protein powder neutral or vanilla
- 80 grams of almond flour
- 70 grams of coconut oil or 90 grams of butter
- 100 grams of xylitol or other sugar substitute
- 1 teaspoon of baking powder
- some water

To finish

4 teaspoons of jam without sugar, bought or homemade

preparation

1. Preheat the oven to 160 degrees top and bottom heat. Mix the dry ingredients together, then add the oil / butter. Gradually add a little water until the dough sticks together when you press it together.
2. Then roll out the dough flat, cut out the desired cookie shape (I took a large and a small heart) and place in the oven until the cookies are golden brown (about 10 minutes). Tip: Bake the hollowed-out cookies and the whole cookies on two different trays, as the hollowed-out cookies are ready faster. Take the biscuits out of the oven and let them cool for about 20 minutes.
3. Briefly heat the jam in a small saucepan (do not boil). Spread the mixture over the biscuits, place the edges on them, wait a little for the jam to dry and enjoy!

Low carb stollen confectionery without sugar and flour

preparation

25 min.

baking time

12 min.

Quantity: 40 pieces

Ingredients

For the dough

- 180 grams of almond flour de-oiled
- 50 grams of ground almonds
- 40 grams of xylitol
- 40 grams of erythritol
- 100 grams of butter soft
- 1 medium-sized egg
- 150 grams of low-fat quark
- 2 teaspoons of stollen spice or cinnamon, cloves, ginger etc.
- 1/2 packet of baking powder
- 1 pinch of salt

To refine

- 70 grams of raisins
- 2 tablespoons of apple juice or rum
- 40 grams of almonds chopped
- 100 grams of low carb marzipan see tip

For painting

- 50 grams of butter, liquid, rough indication
- 40 grams of powdered erythritol powder

preparation

1. Soak the raisins in juice or rum. Preheat the oven to 200 degrees top and bottom heat. Mix the de-oiled almond flour, ground almonds, stollen spice, baking powder and salt.
2. Beat the soft butter with the xylitol and erythritol until frothy, add the egg and quark. Also stir in the dry ingredients briefly. Finally knead the soaked raisins and the chopped almonds into the dough.
3. Cut the marzipan into mini cubes. Shape the dough into long, thin strands on a baking mat or similar. Divide into small portions with a sharp knife. Put a marzipan cube in each piece of dough, shape the dough around it. Place the Stollen Confectionery on a baking tray lined with baking paper and bake for about 12-14 minutes. Do the same with the rest of the dough.

4. As soon as a sheet of Stollen Confectionery is ready, brush it with melted butter while it is still warm and roll it in powder xucker. Let cool and store in a tightly closing cookie jar.

Rhubarb cake with crumble from the tray

preparation

25 min.

baking time

40 min.

Quantity: 1 baking sheet

ingredients

For the sprinkles

- 125 grams of cold butter in pieces
- 125 grams of wheat flour
- 80 grams of ground almonds Amaretti variant see tips
- 70 grams of sugar

For evidence

- 700 grams of rhubarb
- For the dough
- 250 grams of butter soft
- 180 grams of sugar
- 4 medium-sized eggs

* 400 grams of wheat flour
* 2 teaspoons of baking powder
* 1 pinch of salt
* 120 milliliters of milk rough indication

preparation

1. First prepare the crumble. To do this, knead the finely chopped cold butter with the other ingredients briefly with your hands and shape into crumble. Put something into the fridge.
2. Clean, wash, peel and roughly cut the rhubarb stalks into 1-2 cm pieces. Line a baking sheet with parchment paper or grease and dust with flour. Preheat the oven to 175 degrees top and bottom heat.
3. For the batter, beat the softened butter with the sugar until frothy. Gradually stir in eggs one at a time. Finally stir in the flour mixed with the baking powder and salt alternately with the milk. The dough should fall from the spoon with difficulty.
4. Spread the dough on the baking sheet, smooth it out, gently press in the rhubarb pieces and finally spread the crumble on the cake. Bake for about 40-45 minutes.

Healthy vegan children's biscuits without sugar and eggs

preparation

10 min.

baking time

20 min.

Quantity: 35 cookies

Ingredients

- 1 1/2 large apples peeled and grated
- 1 tablespoon of lemon juice
- 120 grams of dried apricots unsulphurized
- 90 milliliters of oat milk, alternatively cow, almond or rice milk
- 90 milliliters of coconut oil or rapeseed oil, I use a 1: 1 mixture
- 270 grams of whole wheat flour or whole spelled
- 180 grams of 5-grain mixture, alternatively just oat flakes
- 1 pinch of salt

preparation

1. Drizzle the grated apples with the lemon juice. Chop the apricots very finely and add. Preheat the oven to 180 degrees top and bottom heat.
2. Mix the milk and oil. Put the flour, flakes, salt and possibly spices in a bowl. Quickly stir in the fruits and the milk-oil mixture (you can also use a simple spatula). The dough should be rather moist. If it is extremely wet, you can add a spoonful of flour.
3. Form small balls with your hands, place them on a baking sheet lined with baking paper and flatten the balls into biscuits. The thinner the batter, the crisper the cookies will be. Bake cookies for about 20 minutes. They tend to stay soft.

Healthy whole meal cookies without sugar and butter

preparation

15 min.

baking time

20 min.

Quantity: 40 cookies

ingredients

- 300 grams of dried fruits e.g., apricots, apples, plums, pineapples
- 2 pieces of oranges organic
- 4 large eggs
- 150 grams of wholemeal spelled flour or whole wheat flour
- 3 teaspoons of baking powder
- 350 grams ground almonds

preparation

1. Finely chop the mixed dried fruits. Wash the oranges, grate and squeeze out the juice. Soak the fruit pieces in the juice overnight (at least 3-4 hours).
2. The soaked fruits with a food processor or similar. puree to a paste (attention, very sticky!). Beat the egg whites until stiff. Mix in the fruit puree and egg yolks alternately on a low level with the food processor.

3. Preheat the oven to 180 degrees top and bottom heat. Mix the flour with the baking powder and sieve on the mass. A small part of the wholemeal flour may remain in the sieve. Fold in the almonds.
4. Shape the dough into small balls with moistened hands. Place on a baking sheet lined with baking paper and flatten gently with your hands or a fork. Bake for around 20 minutes.

Basic recipe for simple gluten-free cookies

preparation

10 min.

baking time

12 min.

waiting period

2 hours

Quantity: 50 pieces

Ingredients

For the dough

- 150 grams of rice flour or other gluten-free flour
- 100 grams of cornstarch
- 40 grams of ground almonds
- 100 grams of xylitol or erythritol or normal sugar

- 150 grams of butter cold and in small pieces
- 2 medium egg yolks
- 1/2 teaspoon of xanthan gum or locust bean gum

To refine

- Chopped pistachio nuts
- Chocolate drops without sugar
- freeze-dried raspberries
- Raisins
- chopped almonds or nuts

preparation

1. Knead all ingredients first with the food processor, then with your hands to form a smooth shortcrust pastry. Divide the dough into several portions as desired and knead in the refining ingredients. Shape dough balls, wrap in cling film and refrigerate for 2 hours.
2. Preheat the oven to 175 degrees top and bottom heat. Line two trays with baking paper. Take the dough balls out of the refrigerator, let them reach room temperature briefly and roll out between foil. Cut out cookies.
3. Bake the cookies for about 10-13 minutes, depending on their size and thickness. Let them cool on the baking sheet as they are still very tender when warm. You can also decorate the cookies if you like.

Ricciarelli: Italian almond biscuits with a soft core

preparation

25 min.

baking time

20 min.

waiting period

30 min.

Quantity: 45 pieces

Ingredients

- 300 grams of almonds ground and peeled
- 1 tablespoon of wheat flour can also be left out
- 1 teaspoon of baking powder
- 4 drops of bitter almond oil
- 200 grams of powdered sugar plus a little dusting
- 2 medium egg whites
- 1 pinch of salt
- 1 teaspoon of grated lemon peel
- 1 teaspoon of baking cocoa optional, for the dark version

preparation

1. Mix the almonds with baking powder, bitter almond oil, half of the powdered sugar and possibly flour.
2. Beat the egg whites with the salt until stiff, sprinkling in the rest of the powdered sugar. Knead the almond mixture into the stiff egg white. I did it with my hands. Warning: the whole thing will be pretty sticky ;-).
3. Halve the dough. Knead the cocoa powder under half of the dough and the lemon peel under the other half.
4. Line a baking sheet with parchment paper. Shape the mixture into long rolls and cut off slices with a sharp knife. Place them next to each other on the baking sheet and press in with the back of the fork to create a pattern. Or shape small balls with your hands and flatten them lightly on the baking sheet. Of course, you can also shape oval biscuits or roll out the almond mixture between two layers of baking paper and cut diamonds.
5. Let the Ricciarelli rest for a good half an hour. Preheat the oven to 120 degrees top and bottom heat. Bake or let dry for around 20 minutes. Very important: the biscuits must still be white and moist! Dust the Ricciarelli with icing sugar, let cool on the baking sheet and then carefully dissolve.

Simple Florentine cookies with almonds

preparation

25 min.

baking time

10 min.

Quantity: 20 pieces

Ingredients

For the cookies

- 120 grams of cream
- 60 grams of butter
- 130 grams of sugar
- 2 tablespoons of honey
- 50 grams of orange peel chopped into small pieces
- 50 grams of lemon chopped into small pieces
- 200 grams of almonds sliced, possibly half sliced
- 25 grams of cornstarch or flour
- 1/2 teaspoon of cinnamon

For painting

150 grams of dark chocolate couverture

preparation

1. Bring the cream, butter, sugar and honey to the boil in a saucepan or pan. Simmer gently over a low heat for approx. 4-5 minutes, stirring, until the mixture is golden brown. Take off the stove.
2. Preheat the oven to 180 degrees circulating air. Line two trays with baking paper. Chop the orange peel and lemon peel very finely. Stir into the butter and sugar mixture together with the flaked almonds, starch and cinnamon. Let everything simmer again over a low heat for 3 minutes.
3. Use a large, round cookie cutter or 2 tablespoons to place heaps a long way apart on the trays. Bake until golden brown for about 9-12 minutes, depending on the size. As soon as the cookies are ready, you should push them back into shape again using the cookie cutter or a glass (which you immerse in water). Let cool down.
4. Melt the couverture in a hot water bath. Carefully brush the completely cooled cookies on the bottom. Place the icing side down on the baking paper and let it set in a cool place

Simple, juicy coconut macaroons: the best recipe

preparation

15 min.

baking time

15 min.

Quantity: 45 macaroons

Ingredients

For the macaroon mixture

- 4 medium egg whites
- 2 pinches of salt
- 150 grams of powdered sugar or sugar
- 200 grams of coconut flakes
- 1 piece of lemon of it juice and zest
- Optional to cover
- 2 pieces of lemon of which juice and zest; for lemon icing
- 200 grams of powdered sugar for lemon icing
- Chocolate icing for chocolate topping

preparation

1. Preheat the oven to 160 degrees top and bottom heat. Line a baking sheet with parchment paper. Beat the egg whites (which really shouldn't contain a trace of egg yolk!) With the salt until stiff. As soon as the egg whites are quite firm, slowly trickle in the sugar while continuing to stir. Continue beating until the egg whites have shiny tips and are completely stiff.
2. Wash the lemon, rub off the zest with a zest, cut in half and squeeze out. Add the juice and the grated zest to the egg whites. Carefully but thoroughly fold in with the desiccated coconut.
3. With two teaspoons or your hands, place about 45 small piles of coconut on the baking paper. Bake the macaroons for around 12 to 15 minutes. They should still be comparatively light and soft. Let cool down.
4. For the coating, rub and squeeze the lemons and mix the juice with the sifted powdered sugar. Brush or coat the macaroons with it. Decorate with zest. Alternatively, dip in liquid chocolate icing.

Vegan chocolate cookies without margarine, butter or egg

preparation

20 min.

baking time

12 min.

waiting period

1 hour

Quantity: 25 pieces

Ingredients

- 200 grams of spelled flour type 630; alternatively normal wheat flour
- 40 grams Linette refined flax seed meal with lots of Omega 3
- 1/4 teaspoon ground vanilla
- 1 pinch of salt
- 30 grams of cocoa
- 60 grams of whole cane sugar, alternatively brown sugar or coconut sugar
- 80 grams of coconut oil
- 50 grams of dark chocolate with at least 70% cocoa content
- 60 grams of banana very ripe

preparation

1. Mix the flour, flax flour, vanilla, salt and cocoa in a bowl. In a second bowl, beat the coconut oil (which should be soft and creamy) with the sugar for a few minutes until frothy.
2. Melt the chocolate in a hot water bath or in the microwave. Mash the banana with a fork to make puree. Add both together with the dry ingredients to the coconut oil-sugar mixture and knead briefly to form a homogeneous dough.
3. Wrap the dough in cling film or similar and chill for about 1 hour. Preheat the oven to 175 degrees top and bottom heat. Cover a tray with baking paper.
4. Shape the dough into small balls and place them on the tray with a little space between them. If you like, you can roll out the dough between two layers of cling film and cut out biscuits.
5. Bake the cookies for about 12 minutes and leave them on the tray for a few more minutes. They are still quite soft right after baking, but get harder when they cool down.

Vegan, low carb & gluten-free 2-ingredient cookies

preparation

10 min.

baking time

12 min.

Cooling time

15 min.

Quantity: 25 pieces

Ingredients

For the dough

- 100 grams of ground almonds blanched
- 30 grams of sugar-free syrup
- Optional to refine
- 1/2 teaspoon vanilla paste
- 1/2 teaspoon lemon paste
- 100 grams of sugar-free jam

preparation

1. First knead the almonds, syrup and a mini shot of water in a kitchen shredder or similar, then knead with your hands. The mass looks very crumbly at first, but becomes

homogeneous through mixing and then kneading and takes on the consistency of marzipan.

2. Shape the dough into a ball and wrap in foil and cool for at least 15 minutes.
3. Preheat the oven to 130 degrees top and bottom heat. Roll out in a cut freezer bag or between foil and cut out approx. 25 small cookies with cookie cutters.
4. Spread on a baking sheet lined with baking paper and bake for about 12-15 minutes, depending on the thickness. Caution: Not too long so that they don't get dry. Decorate or fill as you like.

Vegan coconut macaroons made from 3 ingredients without baking

preparation

10 min.

Quantity: 40 pieces

ingredients

For the coconut macaroons

- 300 grams of coconut flakes
- 170 grams of coconut oil
- 120 grams of rice syrup or agave syrup, honey etc.
- Optional to refine
- Dark chocolate couverture
- ground vanilla
- ground lemon peel

preparation

1. Grind the coconut flakes finer again in the food processor or kitchen chopper. Let the coconut oil melt. Add to the coconut flakes along with the liquid sweetener. Mix everything very well for a few minutes. It is best to add the sweetener little by little and try when the consistency and sweetness that is best for you has been achieved. Possibly flavor with spices.
2. Shape the lukewarm mass into balls with moistened hands; alternatively, press coconut mass into a melon cutter or espresso scoop and carefully tap out. Chill the macaroons. Decorate with couverture if you like.

Vegan cinnamon stars without eggs and egg substitutes

preparation

20 min.

baking time

15 min.

waiting period

4 hours

Quantity: 45 pieces

Ingredients

For the dough

- 200 grams of powdered sugar
- 350 grams of ground almonds
- 1 tablespoon of juice e.g., orange or apricot
- 4 tablespoons of water
- 2 tablespoons of apricot jam or orange
- 2 tablespoons of cinnamon

For the glaze

- 100 grams of powdered sugar
- 1 tablespoon of water roughly indicated, as required!

preparation

1. Knead all the ingredients for the dough. Shape into a ball, wrap in cling film and refrigerate for approx. 1 hour.
2. Roll out the dough half a centimeter thick on a baking mat or between 2 layers of baking paper or a large freezer bag that has been cut open. The dough is very sticky, if necessary, sprinkle some ground almonds on the work surface.
3. Cut out stars. In between dipping cookie cutters in ground almonds or water. Place the stars on 2 baking sheets with baking paper. Let the cinnamon stars dry for approx. 3 hours at room temperature.
4. Preheat the oven to 130 degrees circulating air. Bake cinnamon stars for about 15 minutes. Mix powdered sugar with very little water to form a thick, chewy icing. Brush cooled stars with it.

Clean Eating Christmas cookies to cut out

preparation

20 min.

baking time

12 min.

waiting period

1 hour

Quantity: 40 cookies

Ingredients

For the dough

- 70 grams of coconut blossom sugar, alternatively brown sugar
- 70 grams of coconut oil cool and firm; alternatively, 90g butter
- 50 grams of almond flour
- 170 grams of ground almonds
- 1 piece of vanilla pod
- 1 pinch of salt
- 1 large egg
- 2 tablespoons of ice water
- For decorating
- Chocolate with 75% cocoa
- jam
- Coconut flakes
- Pistachios

preparation

1. Put the coconut oil, which should be rather cool, in small pieces with the coconut sugar in a bowl. Mix well (preferably with a food processor) so that no more pieces can be seen.
2. Halve the vanilla pod lengthways and scrape out the pulp with a teaspoon. Add the remaining ingredients to the coconut sugar mixture and knead everything briefly but vigorously. Shape the dough into two balls, wrap in foil and refrigerate for about 1 hour.
3. Preheat the oven to 175 degrees top and bottom heat. Cover 2 trays with baking mats or baking paper.
4. Roll out the first ball of dough between a large open freezer bag. Cut out biscuits, place on the tray and bake for 12-15 minutes, depending on size or thickness. Do the same with the second ball.
5. Let the cookies cool down and then decorate or fill them with, for example, melted chocolate or jam.

Healthier whole meal butter cookies for Christmas

preparation

10 min.

baking time

12 min.

waiting period

30 min.

Quantity: 30 gr. Biscuits

Ingredients

- 250 grams of whole wheat spelled or wheat flour
- 70 grams of coconut blossom sugar, alternatively whole cane or muscovado sugar
- 150 grams of butter cold and in small pieces

preparation

1. Put the flour and sugar in a bowl. Add the cold butter in small pieces and knead first with the dough hook, then briefly with your hands to form a smooth shortcrust pastry. You may also use 1-2 tablespoons of ice water if the dough is too crumbly.
2. Shape the dough into two balls and wrap them in foil and put them in a cool place for at least 30 minutes. Preheat the oven to 175 degrees top and bottom heat. Cover the tray with baking paper.

3. Roll out the dough in portions and cut out or press into (silicone) molds. Spread on the baking sheet with a little space and bake for 10-15 minutes, depending on the size or thickness. Let cool down well, then remove from the tray.

Basic fruit ice cream recipe:

preparation

10 min.

baking time

10 min.

Cooling time

2 hours

Quantity: 8 servings

ingredients

- 300 grams of fruit e.g., frozen raspberries, see tips
- 120 grams of powdered sugar
- 10 grams of glucose syrup see tip
- 1 teaspoon guar gum or locust bean gum
- 250 grams of cream
- 200 grams of whole milk

preparation

1. Thaw frozen fruits and puree them finely, for example with a food processor or stand mixer.
2. Add all other ingredients and blend in. Put the ice cream base mass in the ice cream machine and make creamy ice cream according to the manufacturer's instructions (for me it takes about 20 minutes).
3. Either enjoy ice cream straight away or put it in the freezer for another 2 hours to solidify. Place in a pre-chilled container with a lid in the freezer to store.

Chocolate pudding

Ingredients for 4 Servings

- 200 g Dark chocolate (approx. 70% cocoa)
- 3 Eggs (size M)
- salt
- 40 g sugar
- 100 g ricotta
- 200 g Whipped cream

preparation

45 minutes

1.

Finely grate about 1 teaspoon of chocolate and finely chop the rest of the chocolate. Preheat the oven for the pudding (electric stove: 180 ° C / convection: 160 ° C / gas: see manufacturer). Melt half of the chopped chocolate over a hot water bath. Separate eggs. Beat the egg white and a pinch of salt until stiff, pour in the sugar and keep beating until it has dissolved. Mix the egg yolks, ricotta, 40 g cream and liquid chocolate. Fold in the egg whites in 2 servings.

2.

Pour the chocolate mass into an oven-safe form (22 cm Ø) and bake in the hot oven for about 25 minutes (see tip).

3.

In the meantime, bring 160 g of cream to the boil for the chocolate sauce. Remove the pan from the heat and melt the rest of the chopped chocolate in the cream while stirring. Drizzle the chocolate sauce over the pudding and sprinkle with grated chocolate. Vanilla ice cream tastes good with it.

4th

TIP: At the end of the cooking time, lightly tap the surface with your finger. If it is just set, the pudding is ready.

High society baked apple with ice cream and meringue crowns

Ingredients for 4 Servings

- 2 Apples (approx. 200 g each; e.g., Boskop)
- 2 tbsp Lemon juice
- 4 tsp sugar
- + 3 tbsp sugar
- 8 (6 g each) "Daim" candies
- 2 fresh egg white (size M)
- salt
- 4 balls (approx. 240 ml) Caramel ice cream
- Parchment paper

preparation

30 minutes

easy

1.

Preheat the oven (electric stove: 200 ° C / convection: 180 ° C / gas: see manufacturer). Halve the apples, cut out the core, drizzle the cut surfaces with lemon juice and sprinkle with 1 teaspoon of sugar each. Place the apple halves on a baking sheet lined with baking paper. Cook in the hot oven for about 15 minutes. Take out and let cool for approx. 30 minutes.

2.

Roughly chop the "Daim" pralines. Beat the egg white and a pinch of salt with the whisk of the mixer until stiff, gradually drizzling in 3 tablespoons of sugar. Place 1 scoop of ice cream in each of the apple halves. Spread the meringue on the ice cream balls with a tablespoon and lightly flame them with a kitchen burner. Sprinkle with pieces of "daim" and serve immediately.

Winter ice bomb with Vin Santo

Ingredients for 10 Servings

- 2 cups (500 ml each) vanilla icecream
- 1 kg Panettone (Italian Christmas Cake)
- 125 ml Vin Santo (Italian dessert wine)
- 3 tbsp, go. good raspberry jam
- 100 g Cherries (glass)
- 75 g candied clementines or other candied fruits
- 1 Organic clementines
- 50 g Pistachio nuts
- 300 g Dark chocolate (70% cocoa content)
- 25 g butter
- Cling film

preparation

20 minutes (+ 720 minutes waiting time)

1.

Let the ice thaw so that it becomes malleable. Line a 2-liter bowl with three layers of foil. Cut 4 round slices (2 cm thick) from the panettone, cut in half. Line the bowl with 6 slices, drizzle with a little Vin Santo. Spread the jam on top.

2.

Drain the cherries. Cut candied fruits into slices. Wash the organic clementine, rub off the peel. Peel the fruit, cut into slices. Spread 1 cup of ice cream on the panettone. Spread the pistachios, cherries and candied fruits on top. Cover with clementine slices. Fill in the rest of the ice. Cover with the rest of the panettone and drizzle with the rest of the Vin Santo. Cover with foil, weigh down with a plate and weight. Freeze overnight.

3.

Turn the ice-cream bomb out about 20 minutes before serving. Chop the chocolate and melt it with butter in a hot water bath. Stir in the clementine peel. Pour some sauce over the ice cream bomb and serve with the rest.

Fluffy quark bowls with chocolate and caramel

Ingredients for 4 Servings

- 500 g low-fat quark
- 2 tbsp Ginger jam (e.g., from Chivers)
- 150 g Whipped cream
- 1 bag (15 g) Gelatin fix
- 80 g fine sugar
- 50 g Caramel sweets (e.g., "Muh-muhs")
- 50 g Dark chocolate

preparation

80 minutes

1.

Put the quark in a damp kitchen towel and squeeze out. Mix with ginger jam. Whip 100 g cream until stiff. Stir Gelatinefix into the quark cream for 1 minute. Fold in the whipped cream, then carefully stir in the sugar. Chill for about 1 hour.

2.

Chop the caramel candies. Heat 50 g of cream in a saucepan and melt sweets in it. Chop the chocolate into coarse shavings. Cut 4 large balls from the quark cream with an ice cream scoop and arrange on plates. Drizzle with the caramel sauce and sprinkle with chocolate.

Espresso rolls with nougat

Ingredients for 8 Servings

- 125 g Nut nougat cream
- 1 pck. vanilla sugar
- 1 tbsp Baking cocoa
- + 60 g + something Baking cocoa
- 400 g Whipped cream
- 3 pck. Cream stiffener
- 5 tsp soluble espresso powder
- 5 Eggs (size L)
- salt
- 125 g + something sugar
- 70 g Flour
- 100 g Hazelnuts
- Parchment paper
- possibly frozen raspberries for decoration

preparation

60 minutes (+ 300 minutes waiting time)

1.

Heat the nut nougat cream in a small pot over low heat. Remove from heat, stir in vanilla sugar, 1 tablespoon of cocoa and 2 tablespoons of cream, let the cream cool for approx. 5 minutes. In the meantime, whip the rest of the cream until stiff, pouring in the cream stiffener. Fold the cooled but still soft nut nougat cream into the cream, chill.

2.

Preheat the oven (electric stove: 220 ° C / convection: 200 ° C / gas: see manufacturer). Line a baking sheet with parchment paper. For the biscuit, mix espresso powder with 4 tablespoons of hot water. Separate eggs. Beat the egg white with a pinch of salt until stiff, while drizzling in 125 g of sugar.

3.

First stir in the egg yolks, then the cooled espresso, into the egg whites. Mix 60 g cocoa and flour, sieve over and fold into the mixture. Spread the dough on the baking sheet. Bake in the hot oven for about 9 minutes. In the meantime, roughly chop the nuts and toast them in a pan without fat.

4th

Remove the sponge cake and immediately turn it over onto a tea towel sprinkled with a little sugar. Carefully peel off the baking paper. Roll up the sponge cake from the short side using the cloth. Let cool down.

5.

Unroll the sponge cake. Spread the filling on the floor, leaving an approx. 2 cm wide border free all around. Spread the nuts on top of the cream, except for 2 tbsp. Roll up the sponge cake again using the cloth. Freeze for at least 4 hours.

6th

Let the Swiss roll thaw for 15-30 minutes before serving. Dust with a little cocoa, garnish with the rest of the nuts and, if desired, with briefly defrosted berries.

Almond tart with a golden nut crown

Ingredients for 8 Servings

- 8th soft caramel candy (approx. 110 g; e.g. "Sahne Muh-Muhs")
- 400 g Whipped cream
- a little + 2 tbsp melted coconut oil
- 150 g dried soft figs
- 200 g Almonds with skin
- approx. 100 g Wild cranberries
- 1 pck. Cream stiffener
- 1-2 tbsp Baking cocoa
- approx. 80 g burnt nuts
- Disposable piping bags with star nozzle (17 mm Ø)

preparation

60 minutes (+ 120 minutes waiting time)

1.

Roughly chop the candy for the cream. Heat with 200 g of cream (do not boil) until the candies dissolve, stirring frequently. Put in a mixing bowl. Stir in 200 g of cold cream. Chill for at least 2 hours.

2.

Grease eight to ten small tartlet molds (approx. 5 cm in diameter) (or grease the hollows of a muffin tin and line each with an approx. 1 cm wide strip of parchment paper). For the base, finely grind figs, almonds and 2 tablespoons of coconut oil in a blender (alternatively in portions in the universal chopper). Press into the mold to form a base, forming an approx. 1 cm high edge. Chill for at least 30 minutes.

3.

Loosen the outer edge of the cooled almond bases with a knife and carefully tip them out of the molds. Stir the lingonberries until smooth and divide into the bowls. Use the whisk of the mixer to whip the chilled caramel cream until stiff, sprinkling in the stiff cream. Fill into a piping bag with a large star nozzle and squirt into the tartelettes as a large tuff. Chill until ready to serve. Garnish with cocoa and roasted nuts.

Orange and caramel flan

Ingredients for 6 Servings

- 1 large organic orange
- 150 g sugar
- + 125 g sugar
- 200 g Whipped cream
- 200 ml milk
- 4th Eggs (size M)
- + 3 Egg yolk (size M)
- 8th shortbread
- freeze bag
- Cling film

preparation

60 minutes (+ 180 minutes waiting time)

1.

Wash the orange with hot water, dry it and finely grate the peel. Halve the orange, squeeze one half. Caramelize 150 g sugar, 4 tablespoons orange juice and half of the orange peel in a saucepan until golden yellow. Immediately divide into six ovenproof molds (approx. 175 ml each) and allow to set.

2.

Preheat the oven (electric stove: 150 ° C / convection: 130 ° C / gas: see manufacturer). Heat the cream and milk (do not boil!). Mix the eggs, egg yolks, 125 g sugar and the rest of the orange peel. Put the biscuits in the freezer bag, close the bag and finely crumble the biscuits with a rolling pin. Mix with the cream milk and add to the egg mixture. Pour into the molds and place on the oven pan (deep baking tray).

3.

Put the drip pan in the oven. Pour in enough hot water until the molds are 2/3 in the water. Let it set in the hot oven for 40–50 minutes. Take out, let cool. Cover and chill for at least 2 hours. Turn out just before serving.

Double Chocolate Pudding with Punch Cherries

Ingredients for 10 Servings

- 1 Organic orange
- 1 glass (720 ml) Sour cherries
- 4 tbsp sugar
- 1 P. vanilla sauce powder (for 1⁄2 l milk; for cooking)
- 1 Cinnamon stick
- 1 pinch according to cardamom
- 100 g Dark chocolate
- 1⁄2 l milk

- 1 packet Chocolate pudding powder

preparation

25 minutes

1.

Wash orange with hot water and rub dry. Peel the peel thinly in a spiral with a peeler. Drain the cherries well in a sieve, collecting the juice. Fill up the juice with water to 1⁄2 l.

2.

Mix 6 tablespoons of cherry juice, 2 tablespoons of sugar and sauce powder until smooth. Bring the remaining juice, cinnamon, cardamom and orange peel to the boil. Stir in the mixed sauce powder, bring to the boil and simmer for approx. 1 minute. Stir in the cherries.

3.

Pour into a bowl and let cool, stirring occasionally. Take out the cinnamon stick and orange peel.

4th

Break the chocolate into pieces. Mix 6 tablespoons of milk, 2 tablespoons of sugar and custard powder until smooth. Bring the rest of the milk to the boil and remove from the stove. Add chocolate and melt while stirring.

5.

Put the pot back on the stove and stir in the mixed pudding powder. Bring to the boil again while stirring and simmer over a low heat for about 1 minute. Immediately fill into four dessert glasses. Spread a few spoons of punch cherries on top.

6th

Serve the pudding warm or cold. Add the remaining cherries.

Two kinds of chocolate mousse with tipsy icing

Ingredients for 4 Servings

- 200 g Whipped cream
- + 100 g Whipped cream
- 2 Eggs (size M)
- 2 tbsp sugar
- 1 pinch (s) salt
- 2 tsp Espresso powder (instant)
- 2 tbsp Orange liqueur (e.g., Cointreau)
- 125 g Dark chocolate

preparation

35 minutes (+ 240 minutes waiting time)

1.

Whip 200 g cream until stiff and chill. Roughly chop the chocolate and melt it in a hot water bath.

2.

Beat eggs, sugar and salt in a metal bowl over the water bath with the whisk of the mixer for about 5 minutes until the mixture warms up. Remove the bowl from the water bath and slowly stir the liquid chocolate into the egg mixture.

3.

Halve the chocolate mass, stir in the espresso powder under one half. Fold in half of the cream and fill the espresso mousse into four glasses (approx. 160 ml each). Fold the rest of the cream into the rest of the chocolate mass, divide into the glasses and chill for approx. 4 hours.

4th

Whip 100 g of cream until stiff and mix 1–2 tablespoons of cream with the liqueur, then fold into the whipped cream with a spatula. Spread the liqueur cream on the mousse and refrigerate until ready to serve. Before serving, decorate with chocolate ornaments as desired.

5.

For the decoration, melt approx. 50 g of chopped couverture and allow to cool a little. Pour the liquid couverture into a freezer bag, cut off a small corner and, for example, sprinkle fir trees and snowflakes on baking paper. Sprinkle with golden sugar pearls and let set in a cool place.

Cheesecake in a baked apple

Ingredients for 4 Servings

- 1 Organic lemon
- 125 g Double cream cheese
- 4 tbsp sugar
- 1/2 tsp Vanilla powder
- 1 Egg (size M)
- cinnamon
- 4th Apples (e.g., boskop)
- 5 tbsp Apple juice
- 100 g Wild cranberries (glass)
- 3 tbsp Sherry or apple juice
- Aluminum foil
- Parchment paper

preparation

45 minutes

1.

Preheat the oven (electric stove: 180 ° C / convection: 160 ° C / gas: see manufacturer). Wash the lemon with hot water, dry it and finely grate some of the peel. Halve the lemon, squeeze out the juice. Mix the cream cheese, lemon zest, 2 tablespoons sugar, vanilla, egg and 1/4 teaspoon cinnamon with a whisk until smooth.

2.

Wash apples, rub dry and cut off a flat lid on top. Carefully remove about 2/3 of the pulp using a spoon or a ball cutter. Leave a margin of at least 1 1/2 cm. Remove seeds and stalk from the pulp and finely chop with the lid. Mix immediately with lemon juice.

3.

Pour the cheesecake mixture evenly into the apples. Wrap the apples tightly with aluminum foil and place on a baking sheet lined with baking paper. Bake in the hot oven for about 25 minutes.

4th

In the meantime, bring 2 tablespoons of sugar to a boil with approx. 1 tablespoon of water and caramelize. Deglaze with apple juice. Add apple pulp, bring to the boil while stirring and simmer for about 1 minute. Take the compote off the stove.

5.

For the sauce, stir together the cranberries and sherry until smooth. Fill the apple compote into four bowls. Place the cheesecake fried apples on top, drizzle with a little cranberry sauce.

That fits Parfait: Chili hearts chocolate

Ingredients for 2 Servings

- 70 g Dark chocolate
- 100 g Whipped cream
- 2 Egg yolk (size M)
- 30 g sugar
- Chili powder
- 1/2 Mango (approx. 200 g)
- 0.5 tsp Vanilla extract
- Sugar hearts to decorate z. B. by Pickerd

preparation

30 minutes (+ 360 minutes waiting time)

1.

Roughly chop the chocolate and melt it over a hot water bath. Whip the cream. Mix the egg yolks and sugar over the hot water bath until thick and creamy. Take off the water bath. Quickly stir in the liquid chocolate and 1 pinch of chilli. Beat over an ice water bath and fold in the cream. Fill the parfait mass into 2 molds (180 ml each) and freeze covered for at least 6 hours, or better overnight.

2.

Peel the mango, cut the pulp from the stone and roughly dice. Puree finely with the hand blender and season with vanilla.

3.

Let the parfait thaw a little or hold the molds briefly in hot water, then tumble out of the molds. Serve with mango sauce and sprinkle with sugar hearts.

Speculoos nice cream with pecans

Ingredients for 4 Servings

- 5 large ripe bananas
- 80 ml Maple syrup
- 1 tsp Baking cocoa
- 6th vegan speculoos (pay attention to the list of ingredients!)
- 60 g Pecans
- 200 ml Almond milk
- Speculoos spice for dusting

preparation

20 minutes (+ 240 minutes waiting time)

1.

Peel the bananas, cut into slices approx. 2 cm thick and freeze for at least 4 hours. In the meantime, stir together the maple syrup and 1/2 teaspoon cocoa. Roughly crumble the speculoos.

2.

Finely puree frozen bananas, speculoos, approx. 40 g nuts, 1/2 teaspoon cocoa and almond milk in a high-performance blender. Layer with 2/3 of the cocoa syrup in glasses.

3.

Serve nice cream with the rest of the nuts. Dust with the speculoos spice and drizzle with the remaining cocoa syrup. Serve immediately